ARTICULATION CURRICULUM I

Jean Gilliam DeGaetano
Illustrated by Kevin Newman

Great Ideas For Teaching!
P.O. Box 444
Wrightsville Beach, NC 28480

Copyright 1987 Great Ideas For Teaching!
All rights reserved. Printed in the U.S.A.
Published by Great Ideas For Teaching!
P.O. Box 444, Wrightsville Beach, NC 28480

Copies of the material may be produced for classroom use
and homework assignments. Copies may not be produced for
entire school districts, used for commercial resale, stored
in a retrieval system, or transmitted in any form; electronic,
mechanical, recording, etc. without permission from the publisher.

ARTICULATION CURRICULUM I

JEAN GILLIAM DEGAETANO

Illustrated by KEVIN NEWMAN

ARTICULATION CURRICULUM I is designed to provide practice for the development or remediation of the following sounds:

b, d, f, g, h, j, k, l, m, n, p, r, s, t, v, w, z, ch, sh, th

The material provides a program for the wide range of articulation errors a speech-language clinician may encounter in a caseload and is appropriate for sound development/remediation on a beginning level through an advanced level.

ARTICULATION CURRICULUM I consists of 120 blackline masters, six masters per sound, and has 1080 illustrations. The directions for class use and for homework are provided at the top of each page, along with a space for the clinician's additional individual instructions. The instructions provide continuity between therapy sessions and home reinforcement practice. Pages are identified by the target sound at the top of each page but left unnumbered to allow more flexibility of use. The word or words under the illustrations provide practice on a beginning level that can easily be changed to more advanced practice by adding words or by using carrier sentences. For example, the words under the illustration may say, "a little letter," but the carrier sentence, "Loopy Lion likes _____," will allow more advanced practice by providing the opportunity to fill in the blank with the word or words under each picture, as "Loopy Lion likes a little letter." Under additional instructions, the clinician can suggest assignments that will emphasize the correct production of the sound, offer the occasion to use the sound in meaningful speech, and stimulate vocabulary development. For example, the additional instruction can state:

"Tell where you might find each thing."

"Tell if each thing is large or small."

"Tell if you have each thing at your house."

"Tell the shape or color of each thing."

"Tell what you can do with each thing."

The desired number of copies of the blackline masters can be duplicated and stored for later use. Booklets can be made for each of the sounds by stapling all of the pages for the same sound together, or the material can be assigned one page at a time. A suggested letter to parents is provided to introduce the sounds. Directions or wording can be modified in any way to assure success in using the material.

VARIATIONS FOR USE

1. The word or words under each illustration can be modified or totally changed to meet the needs of individual students or to provide more practice on specific words or sound positions in words.

2. The pictures can be cut out and mounted on construction paper to make flash cards. The student's goal will be to master the correct production of the sound and to use the words in meaningful speech. This will result in good articulation progress and vocabulary expansion.

3. PICTURE PAIRS Two copies of each illustration are needed for this game. The object of the game is to match alike pictures until all the pictures have been matched in pairs. The pictures can be mounted on tagboard or construction paper to resemble playing cards. Shuffle and deal three "cards" to each player. Place the remaining cards in a stack on the table. The players lay down any matching pairs in their hands. The first player asks any other player for a specific card needed to make a pair. The player must name or describe the picture needed. If that player has the picture, it must be given to the player who asked for it, and play passes to the left. If the other player does not have the card, the player asking for it draws a card from the pile. Play then passes to the left and continues this way until all the cards are matched into pairs. If a player runs out of cards before all the pairs are matched, one may be drawn from the top of the pile.

4. MEMORY MATCHING Two copies of each illustration are needed for this game. The object of the game is to match alike pictures until all the pictures have been matched in pairs. The pictures can be mounted on tagboard or construction paper to resemble playing cards. All the "cards" are spread out, face down, on the table. Taking turns, each player turns up any two cards. If the pictures match (are alike), the player removes them from the table and takes another turn. If the two cards do not match (are not alike), they are turned face down again, and play passes to the player on the left. Play continues until all picture pairs have been matched.

Name _____ Date _____ Sound __b__

In speech class: The word under <u>each</u> picture was said _____ times.
For homework: The word under <u>each</u> picture is to be said _____ times.
Additional instructions: _____
_____

bunny   bird   ball

  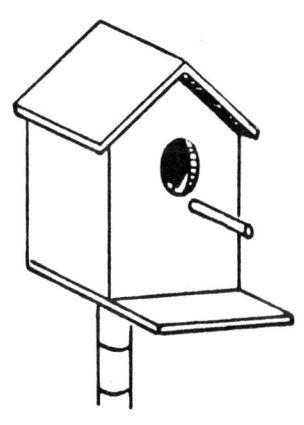

boots   bird nest   birdhouse

  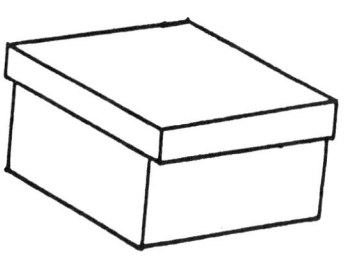

boy   bell   box

Copyright© Great Ideas For Teaching!   <u>ARTICULATION CURRICULUM I</u>

Name _____ Date _____ Sound __b__

In speech class: The words under <u>each</u> picture were said _____ times.

For homework: The words under <u>each</u> picture are to be said _____ times.

Additional instructions: _____
_____

a big bike	a big bell	a big bird
a big barn	a big bird cage	a big bus
a big bear	a big box	big boots

Copyright© Great Ideas For Teaching! ARTICULATION CURRICULUM I

Name _____ Date _____ Sound __b__

In speech class: The words under each picture were said _____ times.

For homework: The words under each picture are to be said _____ times.

Additional instructions: _____
_____

a ball on a barn

a ball on a boy

a ball on a bookcase

a ball on a bed

a ball on a bus

a ball on a boat

a ball on a box

a ball on buttons

a ball on butter

Copyright© Great Ideas For Teaching! ARTICULATION CURRICULUM I

Name _____ Date _____ Sound __b__

In speech class: The words under each picture were said _____ times.

For homework: The words under each picture are to be said _____ times.

Additional instructions: _____
_____

Bobby's boat

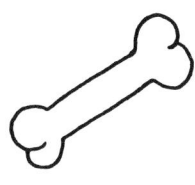

Bobby's bone

Bobby's bee

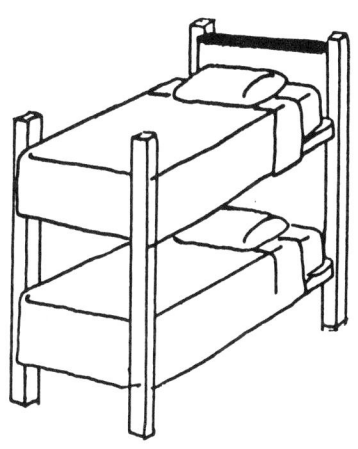

Bobby's bunk beds

Bobby's book

Bobby's barber

Bobby's bat

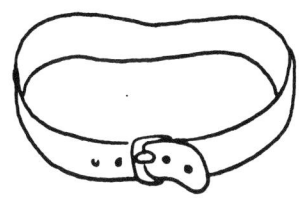

Bobby's belt

Bobby's bus

Copyright© Great Ideas For Teaching!   ARTICULATION CURRICULUM I

Name _____ Date _____ Sound __b__

In speech class: The words under each picture were said _____ times.

For homework: The words under each picture are to be said _____ times.

Additional instructions: _____
_____

a baby

a baby's bib

a baby's bonnet

a baby's boat

a baby's Bear Book

a baby's bear

a baby's bed

a baby's bubbles

a baby's bottle

Copyright© Great Ideas For Teaching!   ARTICULATION CURRICULUM I

Name _____ Date _____ Sound __b__

In speech class: The words under each picture were said _____ times.

For homework: The words under each picture are to be said _____ times.

Additional instructions: _____
_____

web	tub	cab
robe	ice cube	tube
sub	cub	bib

Copyright© Great Ideas For Teaching!   ARTICULATION CURRICULUM I

Name _____ Date _____ Sound __d__

In speech class: The words under each picture were said _____ times.

For homework: The words under each picture are to be said _____ times.

Additional instructions: _____

_____

donkey   duck   door

dam   desk   dog

doll   dirt   deer

Copyright© Great Ideas For Teaching!   ARTICULATION CURRICULUM I

Name _____ Date _____ Sound __d__

In speech class: The word under <u>each</u> picture was said _____ times.
For homework: The word under <u>each</u> picture is to be said _____ times.
Additional instructions: _____
_____

dig

dance

dive

donuts

desert

dice

doctor

daisy

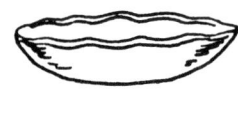
dish

Copyright© Great Ideas For Teaching! ARTICULATION CURRICULUM I

Name _____ Date _____ Sound **d**

In speech class: The words under each picture were said _____ times.
For homework: The words under each picture are to be said _____ times.
Additional instructions: _____
_____

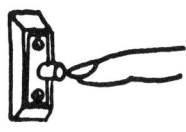
Don's doorbell

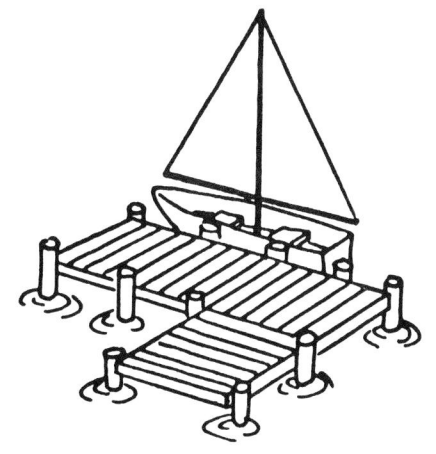
Don's dock

Don's dustpan

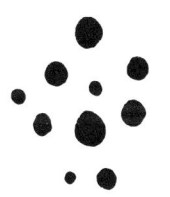
Don's dots

Don's doorknob

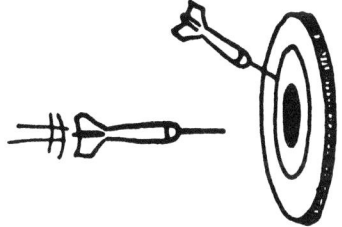
Don's darts

Don's dime

Don's daisies

Don's dishes

Copyright© Great Ideas For Teaching!   ARTICULATION CURRICULUM I

Name _____ Date _____ Sound __d__

In speech class: The words under each picture were said _____ times.

For homework: The words under each picture are to be said _____ times.

Additional instructions: _____
_____

Daddy has candy.

Daddy has a candle.

Daddy has a windmill.

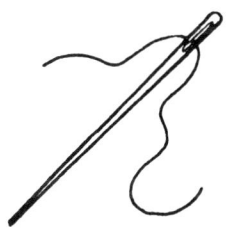
Daddy has a needle.

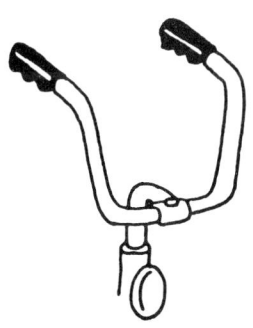
Daddy has handlebars.

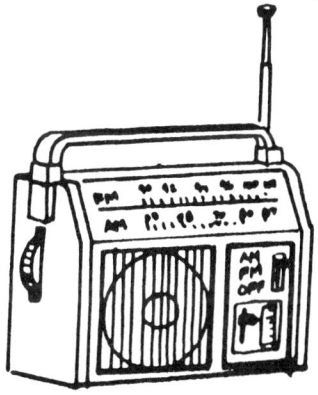
Daddy has a radio.

Daddy has a pedal.

Daddy has a window.

Daddy has a garden.

Copyright© Great Ideas For Teaching!   ARTICULATION CURRICULUM I

Name _____ Date _____ Sound __d__

In speech class: The words under <u>each</u> picture were said _____ times.
For homework: The words under <u>each</u> picture are to be said _____ times.
Additional instructions: _____
_____

dots on a duck

dots on a door

dots on a desk

dots on a dog

dots on a daisy

dots on a devil

dots on a doll

dots on a doctor

dots on a donkey

Copyright© Great Ideas For Teaching!   ARTICULATION CURRICULUM I

Name _____ Date _____ Sound __d__

In speech class: The words under <u>each</u> picture were said _____ times.
For homework: The words under <u>each</u> picture are to be said _____ times.
Additional instructions: _____
_____

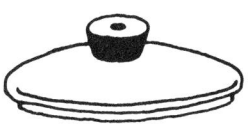

Don sees a lid.

Don sees a bed.

Don sees a card.

Don sees a pad.

Don sees wood.

Don sees a board.

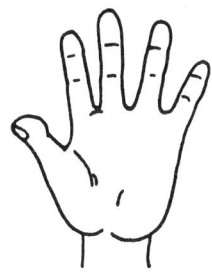

Don sees a hand.

Don sees an ironing board.

Don sees a dad.

Copyright© Great Ideas For Teaching!   <u>ARTICULATION CURRICULUM I</u>

Name _____ Date _____ Sound __f__

In speech class: The word under each picture was said _____ times.
For homework: The word under each picture is to be said _____ times.
Additional instructions: _____
_____

four

fish

fire

fox

five

fan

fairy

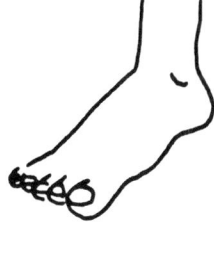

foot

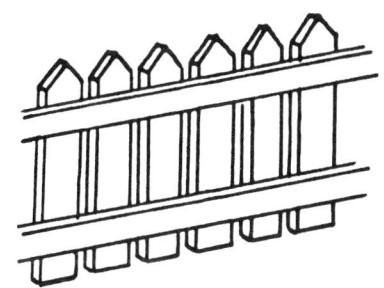

fence

Copyright© Great Ideas For Teaching!   ARTICULATION CURRICULUM I

Name _____   Date _____   Sound __**f**__

In speech class: The word under <u>each</u> picture was said _____ times.
For homework: The word under <u>each</u> picture is to be said _____ times.
Additional instructions: _____
_____

fireplace	fireman	faucet
fire escape	fist	funnel
fishbowl	film	finger

Copyright© Great Ideas For Teaching!   ARTICULATION CURRICULUM I

Name _____ Date _____ Sound __f__

In speech class: The words under <u>each</u> picture were said _____ times.

For homework: The words under <u>each</u> picture are to be said _____ times.

Additional instructions: _____
_____

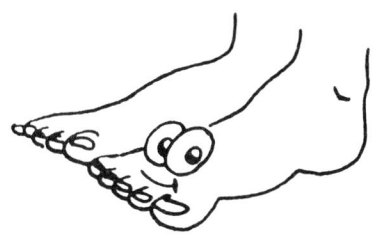
a face on feet

a face on a fire

a face on a fence

a face on a four

a face on a fairy

a face on a fish

a face on a fountain

a face on a fire engine

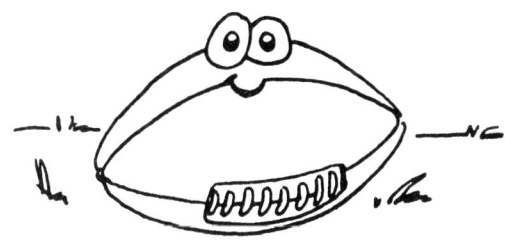
a face on a football

Copyright© Great Ideas For Teaching!   <u>ARTICULATION CURRICULUM I</u>

Name _____ Date _____ Sound __f__

In speech class: The words under each picture were said _____ times.

For homework: The words under each picture are to be said _____ times.

Additional instructions: _____
_____

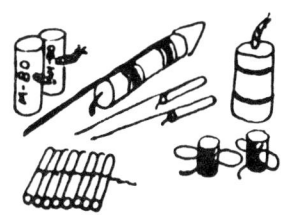

Find fireworks.

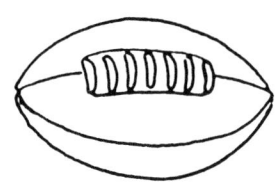

Find a football.

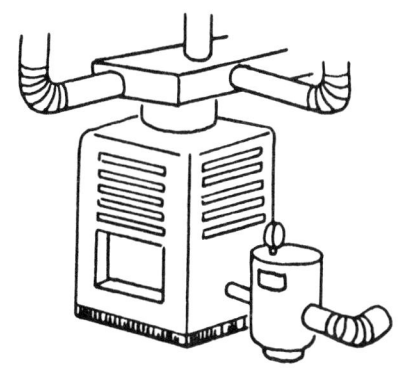

Find a furnace.

Find a fork.

Find a forest.

Find a fan.

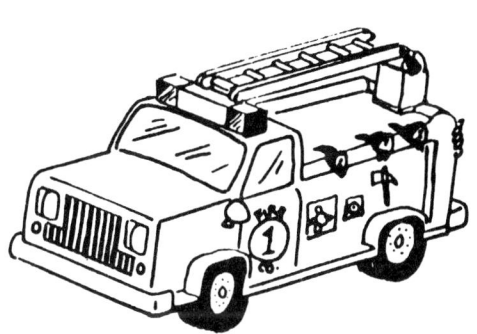

Find a fire engine.

Find a face.

Find a farmer.

Copyright© Great Ideas For Teaching!   ARTICULATION CURRICULUM I

Name _____ Date _____ Sound __f__

In speech class: The words under <u>each</u> picture were said _____ times.
For homework: The words under <u>each</u> picture are to be said _____ times.
Additional instructions: _____
_____

I found a coffee pot.

I found a waterfall.

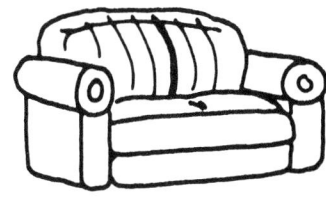
I found a sofa.

I found a waffle.

I found an elephant.

I found a telephone.

I found coffee.

I found a ruffle.

I found a daffodil.

Copyright© Great Ideas For Teaching!   <u>ARTICULATION CURRICULUM I</u>

Name _____ Date _____ Sound __f__

In speech class: The words under <u>each</u> picture were said _____ times.
For homework: The words under <u>each</u> picture are to be said _____ times.
Additional instructions: _____
_____

 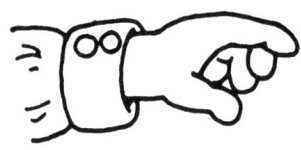 

a funny knife   a funny cuff   a funny elf

  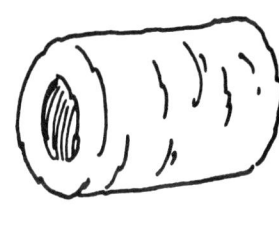

a funny roof   a funny leaf   a funny muff

a funny calf   a funny giraffe   a funny hoof

Copyright© Great Ideas For Teaching!   <u>ARTICULATION CURRICULUM I</u>

Name _____ Date _____ Sound __g__

In speech class: The word under <u>each</u> picture was said _____ times.
For homework: The word under <u>each</u> picture is to be said _____ times.
Additional instructions: _____
_____

girl

gas

gorilla

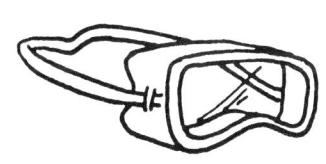
goggles

galoshes

gumdrops

golf clubs

golfer

guitar

Copyright© Great Ideas For Teaching! ARTICULATION CURRICULUM I

Name _____ Date _____ Sound __g__

In speech class: The words under <u>each</u> picture were said _____ times.

For homework: The words under <u>each</u> picture are to be said _____ times.

Additional instructions: _____
_____

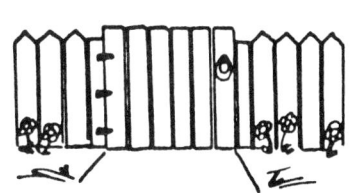

Go to a gate.

Go to a ghost.

Go to a gun.

Go to a goat.

Go to a garage.

Go to a goose.

Go to a gift.

Go to a garbage can.

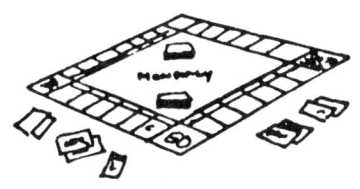

Go to a game.

Copyright© Great Ideas For Teaching! ARTICULATION CURRICULUM I

Name _____ Date _____ Sound __g__

In speech class: The words under <u>each</u> picture were said _____ times.

For homework: The words under <u>each</u> picture are to be said _____ times.

Additional instructions: _____
_____

A ghost saw a hug.

A ghost saw a dog.

A ghost saw a mug.

A ghost saw a pig.

A ghost saw a bug.

A ghost saw a bag.

A ghost saw a wig.

A ghost saw an egg.

A ghost saw a dog beg.

Copyright© Great Ideas For Teaching!   ARTICULATION CURRICULUM I

Name _____ Date _____ Sound __g__

In speech class: The words under each picture were said _____ times.

For homework: The words under each picture are to be said _____ times.

Additional instructions: _____
_____

good girls

good garbage cans

good guns

good gifts

good ghosts

good garages

good geese

good goats

good gulls

Copyright© Great Ideas For Teaching! ARTICULATION CURRICULUM I

Name _____ Date _____ Sound __g__

In speech class: The words under <u>each</u> picture were said _____ times.

For homework: The words under <u>each</u> picture are to be said _____ times.

Additional instructions: _____

_____

Put your finger on
a wagon.

Put your finger on
a hamburger.

Put your finger on
a tiger.

Put your finger on
a finger.

Put your finger on
a merry-go-round.

Put your finger on
a kangaroo.

Put your finger on
a magazine.

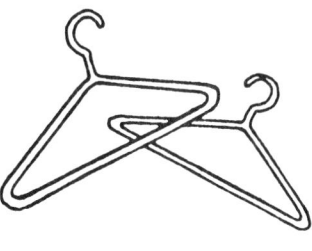

Put your finger on
hangers.

Put your finger on
a target.

Copyright© Great Ideas For Teaching! ARTICULATION CURRICULUM I

Name _____ Date _____ Sound __g__

In speech class: The words under <u>each</u> picture were said _____ times.

For homework: The words under <u>each</u> picture are to be said _____ times.

Additional instructions: _____
_____

Gary's gum

Gary's gas station

Gary's guinea pig

Gary's goalpost

Gary's garden

Gary's gold

Gary's goldfish

Gary's gull

Gary's guard

Copyright© Great Ideas For Teaching!   <u>ARTICULATION CURRICULUM I</u>

Name _____ Date _____ Sound __h__

In speech class: The word under <u>each</u> picture was said _____ times.
For homework: The word under <u>each</u> picture is to be said _____ times.
Additional instructions: _____
_____

hair	heels	horseshoe
haystack	hook	hall
hydrant	handle	horns

Copyright© Great Ideas For Teaching!   <u>ARTICULATION CURRICULUM I</u>

Name _____ Date _____ Sound __h__

In speech class: The word under <u>each</u> picture was said _____ times.
For homework: The word under <u>each</u> picture is to be said _____ times.
Additional instructions: _____
_____

hug	hammock	hit
hide	Humpty Dumpty	hoof
hood	handkerchief	heart

Copyright © Great Ideas For Teaching!   ARTICULATION CURRICULUM I

Name _____ Date_____ Sound __h__

In speech class: The words under each picture were said _____ times.
For homework: The words under each picture are to be said _____ times.
Additional instructions: _____
_____

My hat is here.

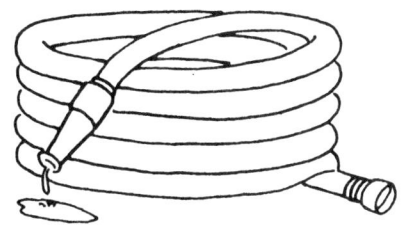

My hose is here.

My hen is here.

My horse is here.

My house is here.

My hair is here.

My hammock is here.

My honey is here.

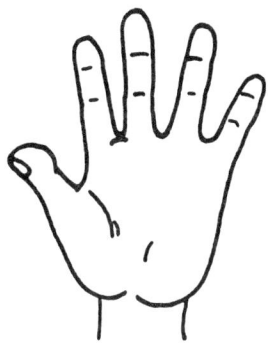

My hand is here.

Copyright© Great Ideas For Teaching! ARTICULATION CURRICULUM I

Name _____ Date _____ Sound __h__

In speech class: The words under each picture were said _____ times.

For homework: The words under each picture are to be said _____ times.

Additional instructions: _____
_____

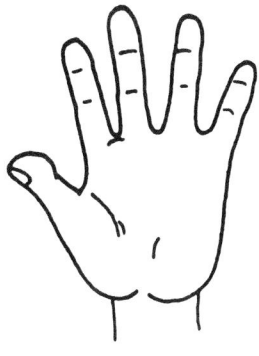

He has a hand.

He has a hat.

He has a hatchet.

He has a helmet.

He has a horn.

He has a hook.

He has a hamburger.

He has a house.

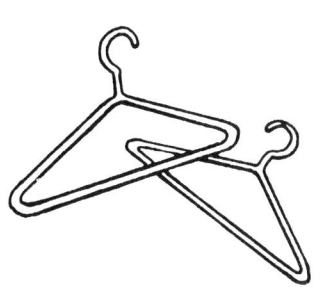

He has hangers.

Copyright© Great Ideas For Teaching! ARTICULATION CURRICULUM I

Name _____ Date _____ Sound __h__

In speech class: The words under <u>each</u> picture were said _____ times.

For homework: The words under <u>each</u> picture are to be said _____ times.

Additional instructions: _____
_____

Hide a harp.

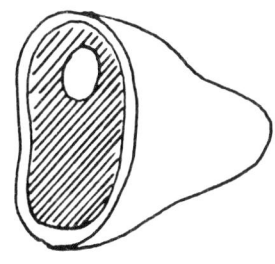

Hide a ham.

Hide a honeybee.

Hide a hat.

Hide a helmet.

Hide honey.

Hide a hamburger.

Hide a hoe.

Hide a hammer.

Copyright© Great Ideas For Teaching!   ARTICULATION CURRICULUM I

Name _____ Date_____ Sound __h__

In speech class: The words under each picture were said _____ times.
For homework: The words under each picture are to be said _____ times.
Additional instructions: _____
_____

Heidi has a clubhouse.

Heidi has a lighthouse.

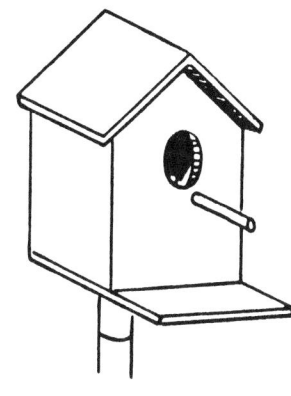
Heidi has a birdhouse.

Heidi has a tomahawk.

Heidi has a rocking horse.

Heidi has a grasshopper.

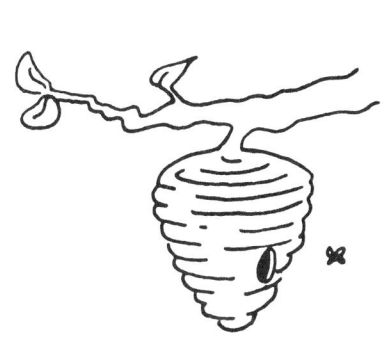
Heidi has a beehive.

Heidi has a tree house.

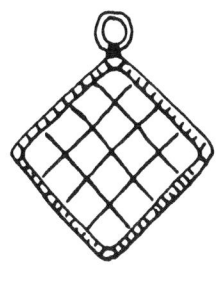
Heidi has a pot holder.

Copyright© Great Ideas For Teaching!   ARTICULATION CURRICULUM I

Name _____ Date _____ Sound __j__

In speech class: The word under each picture was said _____ times.
For homework: The word under each picture is to be said _____ times.
Additional instructions: _____
_____

jug

judge

jeep

jet

jump

jack-o'-lantern

jail

jacket

giraffe

Copyright© Great Ideas For Teaching!   ARTICULATION CURRICULUM I

Name _____ Date _____ Sound __j__

In speech class: The words under <u>each</u> picture were said _____ times.

For homework: The words under <u>each</u> picture are to be said _____ times.

Additional instructions: _____
_____

a "j" on a jug

a "j" on a judge

a "j" on a jeep

a "j" on a jet

a "j" on a jumper

a "j" on a jail

a "j" on a jacket

a "j" on a jack-o'-lantern

a "j" on a giraffe

Copyright© Great Ideas For Teaching!   <u>ARTICULATION CURRICULUM I</u>

Name _____ Date _____ Sound __j__

In speech class: The words under <u>each</u> picture were said _____ times.

For homework: The words under <u>each</u> picture are to be said _____ times.

Additional instructions: _____
_____

Jim's jump rope

Jim's jellybeans

Jim's jam

Jim's jacks

Jim's jack-in-a-box

Jim's jar

Jim's juice

Jim's jack-o'-lantern

Jim's jellyfish

Copyright© Great Ideas For Teaching!   <u>ARTICULATION CURRICULUM I</u>

Name _____ Date _____ Sound __j__

In speech class: The words under each picture were said _____ times.

For homework: The words under each picture are to be said _____ times.

Additional instructions: _____
_____

Jump near pajamas.

Jump near a garbage can.

Jump near an angel.

Jump near oranges.

Jump near vegetables.

Jump near a fire engine.

Jump near a banjo.

Jump near a soldier.

Jump near a blue jay.

Copyright© Great Ideas For Teaching! ARTICULATION CURRICULUM I

Name _____ Date _____ Sound __j__

In speech class: The words under each picture were said _____ times.
For homework: The words under each picture are to be said _____ times.
Additional instructions: _____
_____

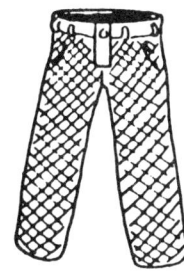
Ginny sees jeans.

Ginny sees a jumper.

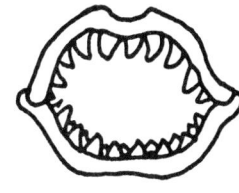
Ginny sees a jaw.

Ginny sees jogging.

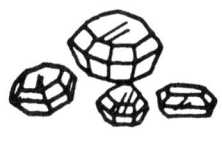
Ginny sees jewels.

Ginny sees jumping.

Ginny sees a juggler.

Ginny sees a gymnast.

Ginny sees a jaguar.

Copyright© Great Ideas For Teaching!　　　　ARTICULATION CURRICULUM I

Name _____ Date _____ Sound __j__

In speech class: The words under each picture were said _____ times.

For homework: The words under each picture are to be said _____ times.

Additional instructions: _____
_____

Jerry's carriage

Jerry's cabbage

Jerry's sponge

Jerry's stage

Jerry's bridge

Jerry's badge

Jerry's orange

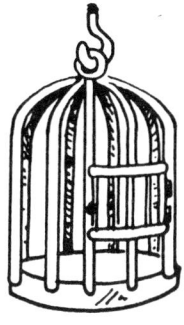
Jerry's cage

Jerry's page

Copyright© Great Ideas For Teaching!   ARTICULATION CURRICULUM I

Name _____ Date _____ Sound __**k**__

In speech class: The word under <u>each</u> picture was said _____ times.
For homework: The word under <u>each</u> picture is to be said _____ times.
Additional instructions: _____
_____

cap	can	king
coat	cut	key
corn	cart	carry

Copyright© Great Ideas For Teaching!   ARTICULATION CURRICULUM I

Name _____ Date _____ Sound __k__

In speech class: The words under <u>each</u> picture were said _____ times.

For homework: The words under <u>each</u> picture are to be said _____ times.

Additional instructions: _____
_____

Katie's cape

Katie's kitten

Katie's cat

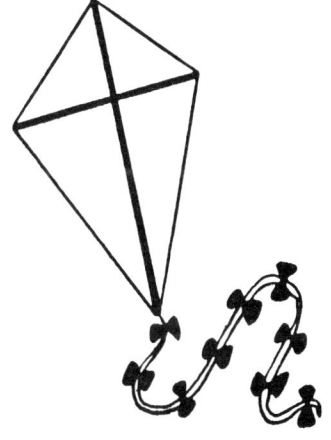

Katie's kite

Katie's kitchen

Katie's camera

Katie's carriage

Katie's cake

Katie's cup

Copyright© Great Ideas For Teaching!   ARTICULATION CURRICULUM I

Name _____ Date _____ Sound __k__

In speech class: The words under <u>each</u> picture were said _____ times.
For homework: The words under <u>each</u> picture are to be said _____ times.
Additional instructions: _____
_____

Kippy's comb

Kippy's camel

Kippy's candy

Kippy's candle

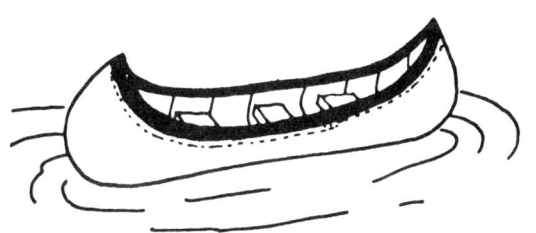

Kippy's canoe

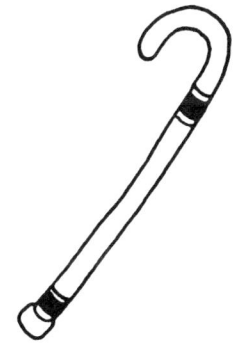

Kippy's cane

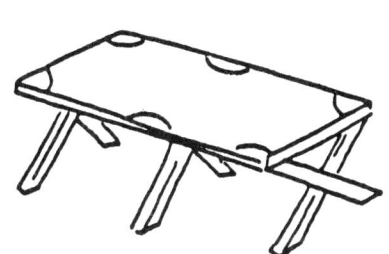

Kippy's cot

Kippy's calendar

Kippy's curtains

Copyright© Great Ideas For Teaching! <u>ARTICULATION CURRICULUM I</u>

Name _____ Date _____ Sound __k__

In speech class: The words under <u>each</u> picture were said _____ times.
For homework: The words under <u>each</u> picture are to be said _____ times.
Additional instructions: _____
_____

Color a garbage can.

Color a monkey.

Color an anchor.

Color popcorn.

Color ice cubes.

Color a pumpkin.

Color a turkey.

Color a donkey.

Color a suitcase.

Copyright© Great Ideas For Teaching!   ARTICULATION CURRICULUM I

Name _____ Date_____ Sound __k__

In speech class: The words under each picture were said _____ times.

For homework: The words under each picture are to be said _____ times.

Additional instructions: _____
_____

Can you color a kangaroo?

Can you color an apple core?

Can you color a car?

Can you color a cow?

Can you color cookies?

Can you color a calf?

Can you color a carrot?

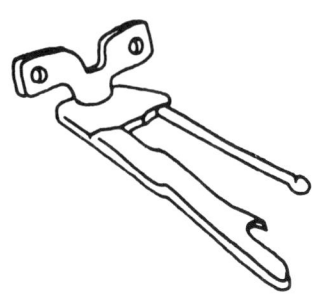
Can you color a can opener?

Can you color a kettle?

Copyright© Great Ideas For Teaching!   ARTICULATION CURRICULUM I

Name _____ Date _____ Sound __k__

In speech class: The words under <u>each</u> picture were said _____ times.

For homework: The words under <u>each</u> picture are to be said _____ times.

Additional instructions: _____
_____

 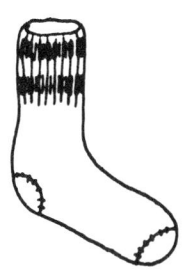 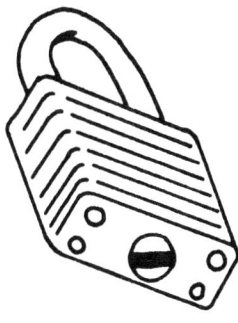

Come see a cake.   Come see a sock.   Come see a lock.

 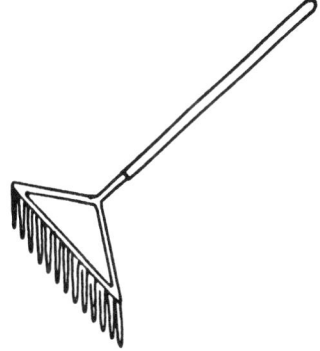 

Come see a book.   Come see a rake.   Come see a tank.

Come see a lake.   Come see a bike.   Come see a rock.

Copyright© Great Ideas For Teaching!   ARTICULATION CURRICULUM I

Name _____ Date _____ Sound __l__

In speech class: The word under <u>each</u> picture was said _____ times.
For homework: The word under <u>each</u> picture is to be said _____ times.
Additional instructions: _____
_____

lamp	leg	ladder
lemonade	lemon	lock
lion	lips	light

Copyright© Great Ideas For Teaching!   <u>ARTICULATION CURRICULUM I</u>

Name _____ Date _____ Sound __l__

In speech class: The word under each picture was said _____ times.
For homework: The word under each picture is to be said _____ times.
Additional instructions: _____
_____

lightning	lettuce	lifeguard
lawnmower	limb	leaf
log	lunchbox	lake

Copyright© Great Ideas For Teaching!   ARTICULATION CURRICULUM I

Name _____ Date_____ Sound __l__

In speech class: The words under each picture were said _____ times.

For homework: The words under each picture are to be said _____ times.

Additional instructions: _____
_____

a little lamb

a little lantern

a little lobster

a little locket

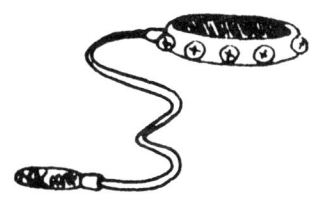
a little leash

a little ladybug

a little lizard

a little letter

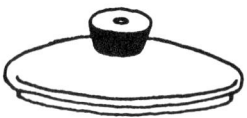
a little lid

Copyright© Great Ideas For Teaching!   ARTICULATION CURRICULUM I

Name _____ Date _____ Sound __l__

In speech class: The words under <u>each</u> picture were said _____ times.

For homework: The words under <u>each</u> picture are to be said _____ times.

Additional instructions: _____
_____

I like a whale.   I like a pail.   I like a pencil.

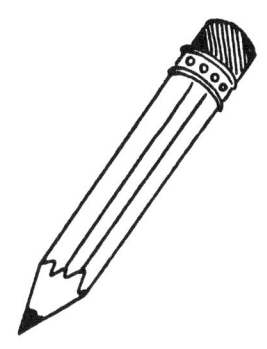

I like a ball.   I like a bell.   I like a towel.

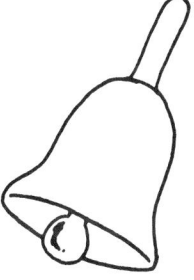

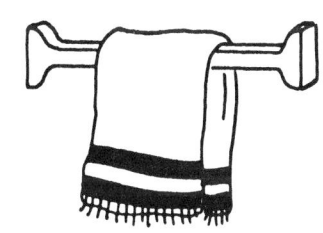

I like an owl.   I like a candle.   I like a camel.

Copyright© Great Ideas For Teaching!   <u>ARTICULATION CURRICULUM I</u>

Name _____ Date _____ Sound __l__

In speech class: The words under each picture were said _____ times.
For homework: The words under each picture are to be said _____ times.
Additional instructions: _____
_____

Look at a balloon.

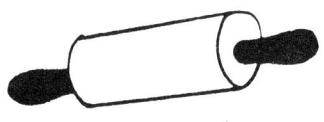
Look at a rolling pin.

Look at an eleven.

Look at a mailbox.

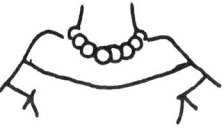
Look at a necklace.

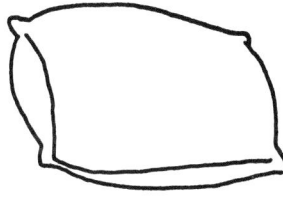
Look at a pillow.

Look at a wallet.

Look at watermelon.

Look at a calendar.

Copyright © Great Ideas For Teaching!   ARTICULATION CURRICULUM I

Name _____ Date _____ Sound __l__

In speech class: The words under each picture were said _____ times.
For homework: The words under each picture are to be said _____ times.
Additional instructions: _____
_____

Leo likes blocks.

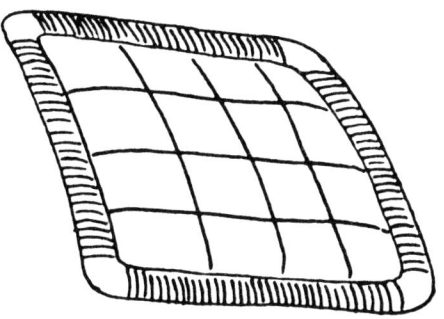
Leo likes a blanket.

Leo likes a flower.

Leo likes a slide.

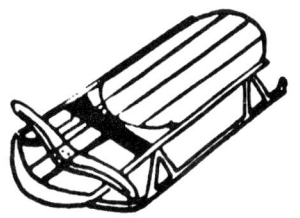
Leo likes a sled.

Leo likes a plate.

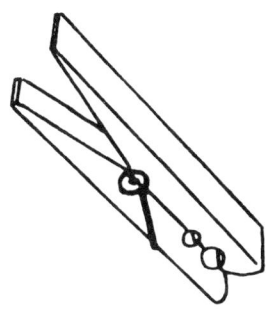
Leo likes a clothespin.

Leo likes a plant.

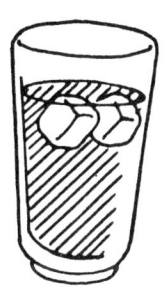
Leo likes a glass.

Copyright© Great Ideas For Teaching!   ARTICULATION CURRICULUM I

Name _____ Date _____ Sound __m__

In speech class: The word under each picture was said _____ times.
For homework: The word under each picture is to be said _____ times.
Additional instructions: _____
_____

meat

monkey

moon

mitten

money

mop

mouse

milk

man

Copyright© Great Ideas For Teaching!   ARTICULATION CURRICULUM I

Name _____ Date_____ Sound __m__

In speech class: The words under <u>each</u> picture were said _____ times.

For homework: The words under <u>each</u> picture are to be said _____ times.

Additional instructions: _____
_____

my map

my mirror

my mail

my mitt

my medicine

my mat

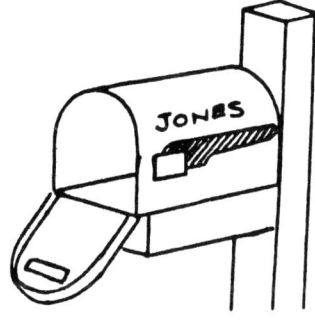

my mailbox

my magnet

my marbles

Copyright© Great Ideas For Teaching! <u>ARTICULATION CURRICULUM I</u>

Name _____ Date _____ Sound __m__

In speech class: The words under each picture were said _____ times.

For homework: The words under each picture are to be said _____ times.

Additional instructions: _____
_____

an "M" on mice

an "M" on merry-go-round

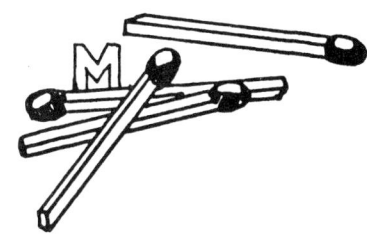
an "M" on matches

an "M" on motor

an "M" on a mint

an "M" on music

an "M" on mud

an "M" on a mixer

an "M" on masks

Copyright© Great Ideas For Teaching!   ARTICULATION CURRICULUM I

Name _____ Date _____ Sound __**m**__

In speech class: The words under <u>each</u> picture were said _____ times.

For homework: The words under <u>each</u> picture are to be said _____ times.

Additional instructions: _____
_____

Mom sees an "M".

Mom sees a match.

Mom sees measles.

Mom sees a mug.

Mom sees a monster.

Mom sees a mattress.

Mom sees a medal.

Mom sees mountains.

Mom sees a mermaid.

Copyright© Great Ideas For Teaching! ARTICULATION CURRICULUM I

Name _____ Date _____ Sound __m__

In speech class: The words under each picture were said _____ times.
For homework: The words under each picture are to be said _____ times.
Additional instructions: _____
_____

Make a mark on a camera.

Make a mark on a windmill.

Make a mark on watermelon.

Make a mark on a hammer.

Make a mark on a lemon.

Make a mark on a camel.

Make a mark on a helmet.

Make a mark on a tomato.

Make a mark on an umbrella.

Copyright© Great Ideas For Teaching!   ARTICULATION CURRICULUM I

Name _____ Date _____ Sound __m__

In speech class: The words under <u>each</u> picture were said _____ times.

For homework: The words under <u>each</u> picture are to be said _____ times.

Additional instructions: _____
_____

my Mama's gum

my Mama's limb

my Mama's comb

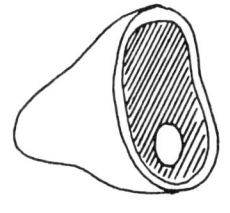

my Mama's ham

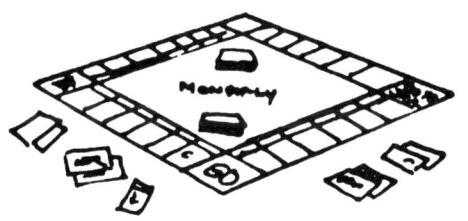

my Mama's game

my Mama's lamb

my Mama's name

my Mama's home

my Mama's worm

Copyright© Great Ideas For Teaching! ARTICULATION CURRICULUM I

Name _____ Date _____ Sound __n__

In speech class: The word under each picture was said _____ times.
For homework: The word under each picture is to be said _____ times.
Additional instructions: _____
_____

| nest | numbers | notebook |

| needle | notes | net |

| nail | necklace | knee |

Copyright© Great Ideas For Teaching!   ARTICULATION CURRICULUM I

Name _____ Date _____ Sound __n__

In speech class: The words under each picture were said _____ times.
For homework: The words under each picture are to be said _____ times.
Additional instructions: _____
_____

a new nine

a new newspaper

a new nut

a new nurse

a new knife

new napkins

a new nightgown

a new net

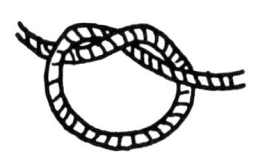

a new knot

Copyright© Great Ideas For Teaching! ARTICULATION CURRICULUM I

Name _____ Date _____ Sound __n__

In speech class: The words under <u>each</u> picture were said _____ times.

For homework: The words under <u>each</u> picture are to be said _____ times.

Additional instructions: _____
_____

an "n" on numbers

an "n" on a nut

an "n" on a nest

an "n" on a nail

an "n" on a newspaper

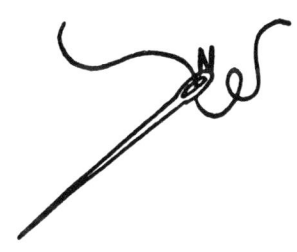

an "n" on a needle

an "n" on a knife

an "n" on a notebook

an "n" on a net

Copyright© Great Ideas For Teaching!   ARTICULATION CURRICULUM I

Name _____ Date _____ Sound __n__

In speech class: The words under each picture were said _____ times.

For homework: The words under each picture are to be said _____ times.

Additional instructions: _____
_____

Nancy sees a nose.

Nancy sees a nun.

Nancy sees a nurse.

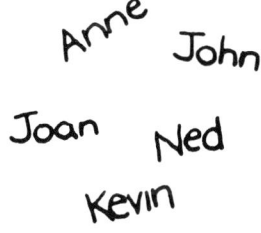

Nancy sees names.

Nancy sees night.

Nancy sees a nap.

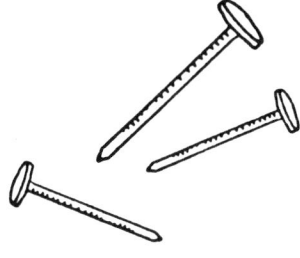

Nancy sees nails.

Nancy sees "NO!"

Nancy sees a neck.

Copyright© Great Ideas For Teaching!   ARTICULATION CURRICULUM I

Name _____ Date _____ Sound __n__

In speech class: The words under each picture were said _____ times.

For homework: The words under each picture are to be said _____ times.

Additional instructions: _____
_____

Nina's pony

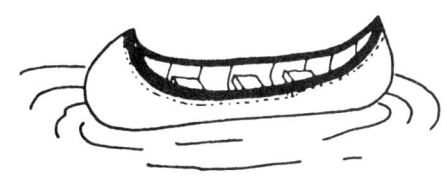
Nina's canoe

Nina's banana

Nina's window

Nina's money

Nina's pineapple

Nina's piano

Nina's tunnel

Nina's candy

Copyright© Great Ideas For Teaching! ARTICULATION CURRICULUM I

Name _____ Date _____ Sound __n__

In speech class: The words under each picture were said _____ times.

For homework: The words under each picture are to be said _____ times.

Additional instructions: _____
_____

Do not circle can.

Do not circle rain.

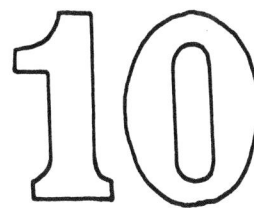

Do not circle ten.

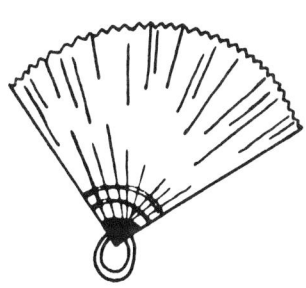

Do not circle fan.

Do not circle barn.

Do not circle pin.

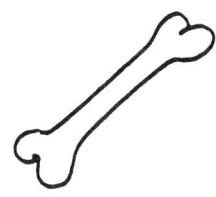

Do not circle bone.

Do not circle man.

Do not circle pan.

Copyright© Great Ideas For Teaching!   ARTICULATION CURRICULUM I

Name _____ Date _____ Sound __p__

In speech class: The word under <u>each</u> picture was said _____ times.
For homework: The word under <u>each</u> picture is to be said _____ times.
Additional instructions: _____
_____

| pull | pack | painter |

| pipe | paint | pad |

| pocket | purse | parachute |

Copyright© Great Ideas For Teaching!   <u>ARTICULATION CURRICULUM I</u>

Name _____ Date _____ Sound __p__

In speech class: The word under each picture was said _____ times.
For homework: The word under each picture is to be said _____ times.
Additional instructions: _____
_____

push

pie

point

pumpkin

pitcher

pail

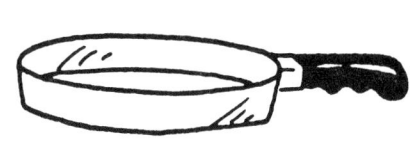
pan

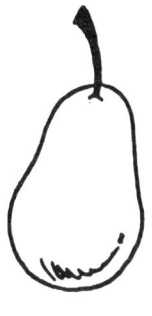
pear

pencil

Copyright© Great Ideas For Teaching!   ARTICULATION CURRICULUM I

Name _____ Date_____ Sound __p__

In speech class: The words under each picture were said _____ times.
For homework: The words under each picture are to be said _____ times.
Additional instructions: _____
_____

Point to pony.   Point to patch.   Point to parakeet.

Point to pen.   Point to parrot.   Point to pin.

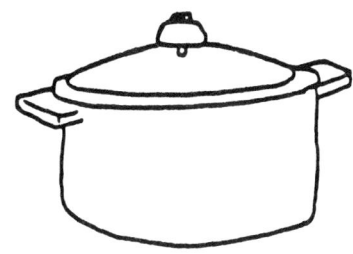  

Point to pot.   Point to pig.   Point to potato.

Copyright© Great Ideas For Teaching!   ARTICULATION CURRICULUM I

Name _____ Date _____ Sound __p__

In speech class: The words under each picture were said _____ times.
For homework: The words under each picture are to be said _____ times.
Additional instructions: _____
_____

Pam's pajamas

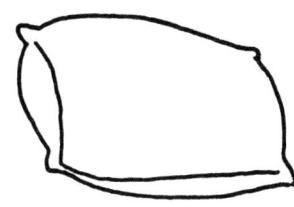
Pam's pillow

Pam's pencil sharpener

Pam's piano

Pam's peanut butter

Pam's peacock

Pam's penguin

Pam's peas

Pam's peach

Copyright© Great Ideas For Teaching!   ARTICULATION CURRICULUM I

Name _____ Date_____ Sound __p__

In speech class: The words under each picture were said _____ times.
For homework: The words under each picture are to be said _____ times.
Additional instructions: _____
_____

Paint a puppet.

Paint a pineapple.

Paint a pigpen.

Paint pumpkins.

Paint popcorn.

Paint a newspaper.

Paint an apple.

Paint a puppy.

Paint a woodpecker.

Copyright© Great Ideas For Teaching! ARTICULATION CURRICULUM I

Name _____ Date _____ Sound __p__

In speech class: The words under each picture were said _____ times.
For homework: The words under each picture are to be said _____ times.
Additional instructions: _____
_____

a "p" on a cap

a "p" on a cup

a "p" on a lamp

a "p" on a rope

a "p" on soup

a "p" on a mop

a "p" on soap

a "p" on tape

a "p" on map

Copyright© Great Ideas For Teaching!   ARTICULATION CURRICULUM I

Name _____ Date _____ Sound __r__

In speech class: The word under each picture was said _____ times.
For homework: The word under each picture is to be said _____ times.
Additional instructions: _____
_____

rain   rope   rat

rose   road   roof

robe   ring   rug

Copyright© Great Ideas For Teaching!   ARTICULATION CURRICULUM I

Name _____ Date _____ Sound __r__

In speech class: The word under <u>each</u> picture was said _____ times.

For homework: The word under <u>each</u> picture is to be said _____ times.

Additional instructions: _____
_____

ruler	ribbon	rake
razor	rattle	rock
rocking chair	rolling pin	roots

Copyright© Great Ideas For Teaching!   <u>ARTICULATION CURRICULUM I</u>

Name _____ Date _____ Sound __r__

In speech class: The words under <u>each</u> picture were said _____ times.
For homework: The words under <u>each</u> picture are to be said _____ times.
Additional instructions: _____
_____

Ride has an "r" sound.

Rock has an "r" sound.

Rip has an "r" sound.

Run has an "r" sound.

Read has an "r" sound.

Write has an "r" sound.

Rake has an "r" sound.

Row has an "r" sound.

Rest has an "r" sound.

Copyright© Great Ideas For Teaching!   ARTICULATION CURRICULUM I

Name _____ Date _____ Sound __r__

In speech class: The words under <u>each</u> picture were said _____ times.

For homework: The words under <u>each</u> picture are to be said _____ times.

Additional instructions: _____
_____

Randy has a robot.

Randy has roller skates.

Randy has a rocket.

Randy has a raincoat.

Randy has a rooster.

Randy has a raccoon.

Randy has a reindeer.

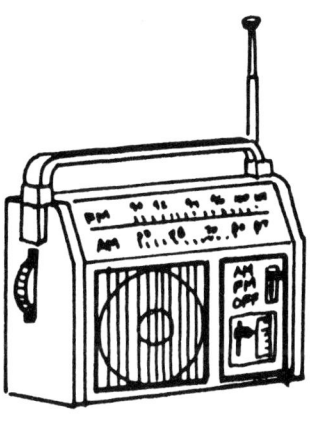
Randy has a radio.

Randy has a rabbit.

Copyright© Great Ideas For Teaching!   ARTICULATION CURRICULUM I

Name _____ Date _____ Sound __r__

In speech class: The words under <u>each</u> picture were said _____ times.

For homework: The words under <u>each</u> picture are to be said _____ times.

Additional instructions: _____
_____

Robin wants cherries.

Robin wants a kangaroo.

Robin wants a carrot.

Robin wants a parrot.

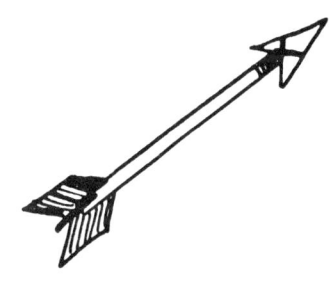

Robin wants an arrow.

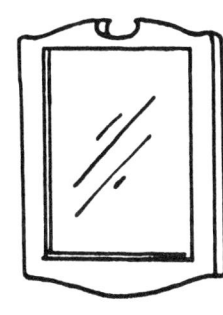

Robin wants a mirror.

Robin wants a fairy.

Robin wants a merry-go-round.

Robin wants a carriage.

Copyright© Great Ideas For Teaching!   ARTICULATION CURRICULUM I

Name _____ Date_____ Sound __r__

In speech class: The words under <u>each</u> picture were said _____ times.

For homework: The words under <u>each</u> picture are to be said _____ times.

Additional instructions: _____

_____

Put a ring around a truck.

Put a ring around a broom.

Put a ring around a frog.

Put a ring around a cross.

Put a ring around a pretzel.

Put a ring around a tree.

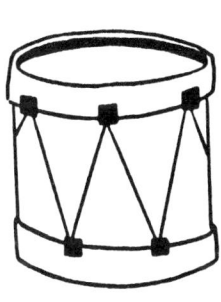
Put a ring around a drum.

Put a ring around a train.

Put a ring around grapes.

Copyright© Great Ideas For Teaching!   <u>ARTICULATION CURRICULUM I</u>

Name _____ Date _____ Sound __S__

In speech class: The word under each picture was said _____ times.
For homework: The word under each picture is to be said _____ times.
Additional instructions: _____
_____

sun	sock	seal
soup	saw	sink

safe

sandwich

saddle

Copyright© Great Ideas For Teaching!   ARTICULATION CURRICULUM I

Name _____ Date _____ Sound __S__

In speech class: The words under <u>each</u> picture were said _____ times.

For homework: The words under <u>each</u> picture are to be said _____ times.

Additional instructions: _____

_____

 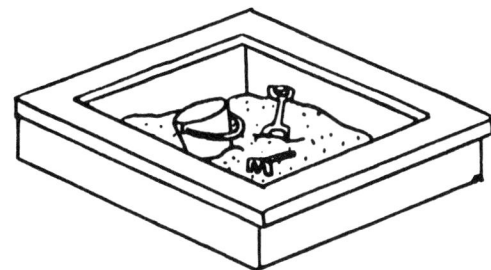 

See a six.   See a sandbox.   See soap.

See a suit.   See a sign.   See Santa.

See sand.   See a seven.   See a sailor.

Copyright© Great Ideas For Teaching!   ARTICULATION CURRICULUM I

Name _____ Date _____ Sound __S__

In speech class: The words under each picture were said _____ times.

For homework: The words under each picture are to be said _____ times.

Additional instructions: _____
_____

Sam saw a snowman.

Sam saw a snake.

Sam saw a star.

Sam saw a stove.

Sam saw a swimmer.

Sam saw a spider.

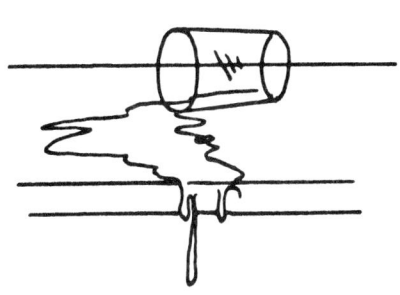

Sam saw a spill.

Sam saw spray.

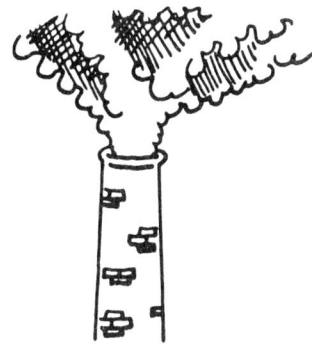

Sam saw smoke.

Copyright© Great Ideas For Teaching!   ARTICULATION CURRICULUM I

Name _____ Date _____ Sound __S__

In speech class: The words under <u>each</u> picture were said _____ times.
For homework: The words under <u>each</u> picture are to be said _____ times.
Additional instructions: _____
_____

Sue sat by a slide.

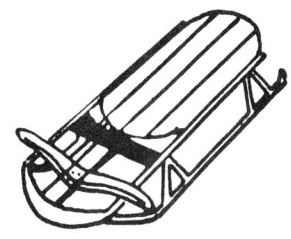

Sue sat by a sled.

Sue sat by a skate.

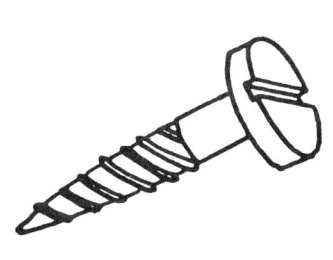

Sue sat by a screw.

Sue sat by a scarecrow.

Sue sat by a street

Sue sat by a squirrel.

Sue sat by strawberries.

Sue sat by a swing.

Copyright© Great Ideas For Teaching!   <u>ARTICULATION CURRICULUM I</u>

Name _____ Date_____ Sound __S__

In speech class: The words under each picture were said _____ times.

For homework: The words under each picture are to be said _____ times.

Additional instructions: _____
_____

Basket has an "s" sound.

Grasshopper has an "s" sound.

Mixer has an "s" sound.

Whistle has an "s" sound.

Mousetrap has an "s" sound.

Pencil has an "s" sound.

Swimsuit has an "s" sound.

Gas station has an "s" sound.

Bicycle has an "s" sound.

Copyright© Great Ideas For Teaching!   ARTICULATION CURRICULUM I

Name _____ Date _____ Sound __S__

In speech class: The words under <u>each</u> picture were said _____ times.
For homework: The words under <u>each</u> picture are to be said _____ times.
Additional instructions: _____
_____

Cindy sees a horse.

Cindy sees a nurse.

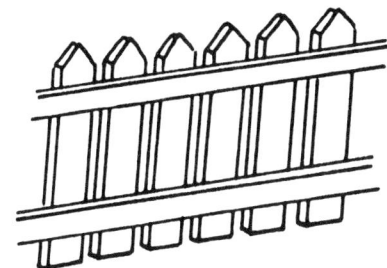
Cindy sees a fence.

Cindy sees a walrus

Cindy sees some jacks.

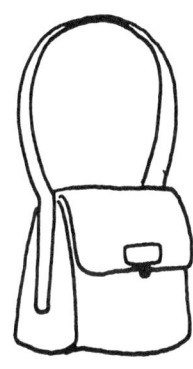
Cindy sees a purse.

Cindy sees an octopus

Cindy sees a lighthouse.

Cindy sees a suitcase.

Copyright© Great Ideas For Teaching!   <u>ARTICULATION CURRICULUM I</u>

Name _____ Date _____ Sound __t__

In speech class: The word under each picture was said _____ times.
For homework: The word under each picture is to be said _____ times.
Additional instructions: _____
_____

"t"

tack

tulip

tie

toes

two

tail

tire

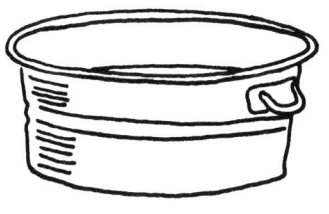
tub

Copyright © Great Ideas For Teaching! ARTICULATION CURRICULUM I

Name _____ Date _____ Sound __t__

In speech class: The word under <u>each</u> picture was said _____ times.
For homework: The word under <u>each</u> picture is to be said _____ times.
Additional instructions: _____
_____

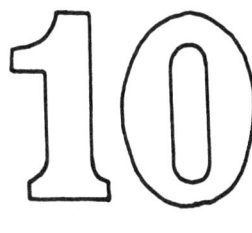

ten

toys

tacks

taxi

ties

tag

table

tape

toe

Copyright© Great Ideas For Teaching!   <u>ARTICULATION CURRICULUM I</u>

Name _____ Date _____ Sound __t__

In speech class: The words under each picture were said _____ times.

For homework: The words under each picture are to be said _____ times.

Additional instructions: _____
_____

a "2" on a top

a "2" on a toast

a "2" on a tire

a "2" on a teapot

a "2" on a tent

a "2" on a tag

a "2" on a tie

a "2" on a tub

a "2" on a target

Copyright© Great Ideas For Teaching!   ARTICULATION CURRICULUM I

Name _____ Date _____ Sound __t__

In speech class: The words under <u>each</u> picture were said _____ times.

For homework: The words under <u>each</u> picture are to be said _____ times.

Additional instructions: _____
_____

Tommy's toys

Tommy's turkey

Tommy's tiger

Tommy's tadpole

Tommy's tepee

Tommy's toad

Tommy's top

Tommy's tank

Tommy's towel

Copyright© Great Ideas For Teaching!   <u>ARTICULATION CURRICULUM I</u>

Name _____ Date _____ Sound __t__

In speech class: The words under each picture were said _____ times.

For homework: The words under each picture are to be said _____ times.

Additional instructions: _____
_____

Talk about mittens.   Talk about butter.   Talk about a doctor.

   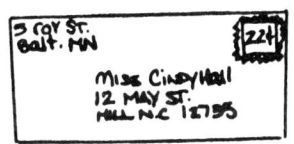   

Talk about a painter.   Talk about a letter.   Talk about pigtails.

Talk about a bow tie.   Talk about a rattle.   Talk about mountains.

Copyright© Great Ideas For Teaching!   ARTICULATION CURRICULUM I

Name _____ Date _____ Sound __t__

In speech class: The words under <u>each</u> picture were said _____ times.

For homework: The words under <u>each</u> picture are to be said _____ times.

Additional instructions: _____
_____

a "t" on a kite

a "t" on a pot

a "t" on a net

a "t" on a coat

a "t" on a boat

a "t" on a bat

a"t" on a hat

a "t" on a heart

a "t" on a boot

Copyright© Great Ideas For Teaching!   <u>ARTICULATION CURRICULUM I</u>

Name _____ Date _____ Sound __V__

In speech class: The word under each picture was said _____ times.
For homework: The word under each picture is to be said _____ times.
Additional instructions: _____
_____

vampire

vest

valentine

vine

vase

vacuum

"v"

vegetables

van

Copyright© Great Ideas For Teaching!   ARTICULATION CURRICULUM I

Name _____ Date _____ Sound __V__

In speech class: The words under each picture were said _____ times.

For homework: The words under each picture are to be said _____ times.

Additional instructions: _____
_____

a "v" on a vase

a "v" on a valentine box

a "v" on a volcano

a "v" on a vest

a "v" on a van

a "v" on a valentine

a "v" on a vulture

a "v" on a violin

a "v" on a vacuum

Copyright© Great Ideas For Teaching!   ARTICULATION CURRICULUM I

Name _____ Date_____ Sound __V__

In speech class: The words under each picture were said _____ times.

For homework: The words under each picture are to be said _____ times.

Additional instructions: _____
_____

very nice valentines

very nice volcanos

very nice vans

very nice vases

very nice violets

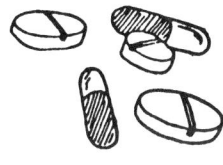

very nice vitamins

very nice vacuums

very nice vests

very nice vampires

Copyright© Great Ideas For Teaching!   ARTICULATION CURRICULUM I

Name _____ Date _____ Sound __V__

In speech class: The words under each picture were said _____ times.
For homework: The words under each picture are to be said _____ times.
Additional instructions: _____
_____

Vera's veil

Vera's vote

Vera's valentine box

Vera's violin

Vera's vowels

Vera's violet

Vera's village

Vera's vulture

Vera's volcano

Copyright© Great Ideas For Teaching!   ARTICULATION CURRICULUM I

Name _____ Date _____ Sound __V__

In speech class: The words under <u>each</u> picture were said _____ times.

For homework: The words under <u>each</u> picture are to be said _____ times.

Additional instructions: _____

_____

A vampire bit a shovel.

A vampire bit a moving van.

A vampire bit an oven.

A vampire bit a seven.

A vampire bit a television.

A vampire bit an eleven.

A vampire bit a beaver.

A vampire bit an envelope.

A vampire bit a movie.

Copyright© Great Ideas For Teaching!   ARTICULATION CURRICULUM I

Name _____ Date _____ Sound __V__

In speech class: The words under each picture were said _____ times.
For homework: The words under each picture are to be said _____ times.
Additional instructions: _____
_____

I have a stove.

I have a five.

I have a sleeve.

I have a cave.

I have a twelve.

I have a beehive.

I have a glove.

I have a dive.

I have a wave.

Copyright© Great Ideas For Teaching!   ARTICULATION CURRICULUM I

Name _____ Date _____ Sound __W__

In speech class: The word under each picture was said _____ times.
For homework: The word under each picture is to be said _____ times.
Additional instructions: _____
_____

wig	watch	window
walrus	windmill	worm
witch	wagon	wood

Copyright© Great Ideas For Teaching! ARTICULATION CURRICULUM I

Name _____ Date _____ Sound __W__

In speech class: The word under each picture was said _____ times.
For homework: The word under each picture is to be said _____ times.
Additional instructions: _____
_____

weep	wade	walk
wash	wink	water
woman	well	wings

Copyright© Great Ideas For Teaching!   ARTICULATION CURRICULUM I

Name _____ Date _____ Sound __W__

In speech class: The words under each picture were said _____ times.
For homework: The words under each picture are to be said _____ times.
Additional instructions: _____
_____

a wet wagon

a wet windmill

a wet witch

a wet wing

a wet worm

a wet walrus

a wet well

a wet window

wet wood

Copyright© Great Ideas For Teaching! ARTICULATION CURRICULUM I

Name _____ Date_____ Sound __W__

In speech class: The words under each picture were said _____ times.

For homework: The words under each picture are to be said _____ times.

Additional instructions: _____
_____

I want a wolf.   I want words.   I want the world.

I want a wand.   I want a wastebasket.   I want a water gun.

I want a watermelon.   I want a waterfall.   I want a welcome mat.

Copyright© Great Ideas For Teaching!   ARTICULATION CURRICULUM I

Name _____ Date _____ Sound __W__

In speech class: The words under each picture were said _____ times.

For homework: The words under each picture are to be said _____ times.

Additional instructions: _____
_____

Wanda's one

Wanda's woodpecker

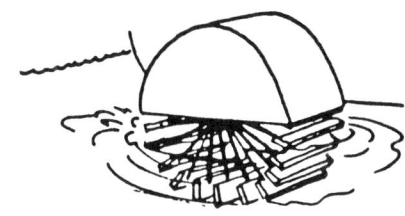

Wanda's waterwheel

Wanda's walnuts

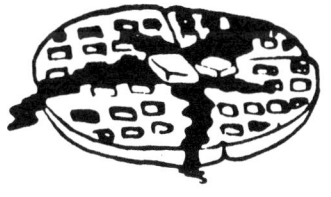

Wanda's waffles

Wanda's wallet

Wanda's web

Wanda's workbench

Wanda's waitress

Copyright© Great Ideas For Teaching!   ARTICULATION CURRICULUM I

Name _____ Date _____ Sound __W__

In speech class: The words under <u>each</u> picture were said _____ times.
For homework: The words under <u>each</u> picture are to be said _____ times.
Additional instructions: _____
_____

Wendy wants a thirty-one.

Wendy wants a sandwich.

Wendy wants a "Bow-Wow" dog.

Wendy wants a stopwatch.

Wendy wants a wigwam.

Wendy wants a wooden wagon.

Wendy wants a wishing well.

Wendy wants a spillway.

Wendy wants a tower wall.

Copyright© Great Ideas For Teaching!   ARTICULATION CURRICULUM I

Name _____ Date _____ Sound __Z__

In speech class: The word under each picture was said _____ times.
For homework: The word under each picture is to be said _____ times.
Additional instructions: _____
_____

zinnia

zigzag

zero

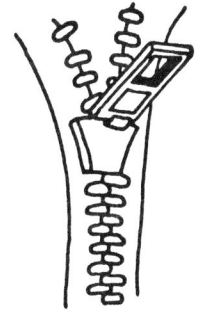
zipper

zip code

zebra

zoo cage

zoo keeper

xylophone

Copyright© Great Ideas For Teaching!　　　ARTICULATION CURRICULUM I

Name _____ Date_____ Sound __Z__

In speech class: The words under each picture were said _____ times.

For homework: The words under each picture are to be said _____ times.

Additional instructions: _____
_____

Zane can draw a zinnia.

Zane can draw a zigzag.

Zane can draw a zero.

Zane can draw a zipper.

Zane can draw a zip code.

Zane can draw a zebra.

Zane can draw a zoo cage.

Zane can draw a zoo keeper.

Zane can draw a xylophone.

Copyright© Great Ideas For Teaching!   ARTICULATION CURRICULUM I

Name _____ Date _____ Sound __Z__

In speech class: The words under each picture were said _____ times.

For homework: The words under each picture are to be said _____ times.

Additional instructions: _____
_____

Zippy has a zinnia.

Zippy has a zigzag.

Zippy has a zero.

Zippy has a zipper.

Zippy has a zip code.

Zippy has a zebra.

Zippy has a zoo cage.

Zippy has a zoo keeper.

Zippy has a xylophone.

Copyright© Great Ideas For Teaching!   ARTICULATION CURRICULUM I

Name _____ Date _____ Sound __Z__

In speech class: The words under each picture were said _____ times.
For homework: The words under each picture are to be said _____ times.
Additional instructions: _____
_____

a "z" on music

a "z" on measles

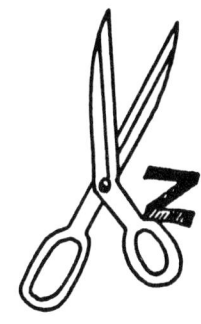

a "z" on scissors

a "z" on buzzer

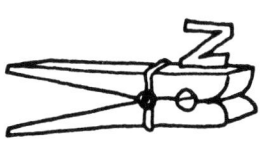

a "z" on clothespin

a "z" on dessert

a "z" on present

a "z" on razor

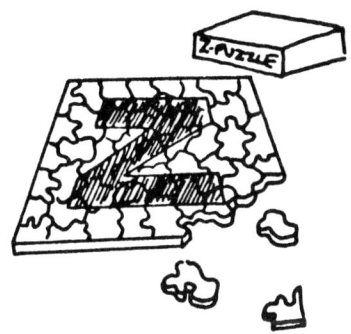

a "z" on puzzle

Copyright© Great Ideas For Teaching!   ARTICULATION CURRICULUM I

Name _____ Date _____ Sound __Z__

In speech class: The word under each picture was said _____ times.
For homework: The word under each picture is to be said _____ times.
Additional instructions: _____
_____

zinnias	zigzags	zeros
zippers	zip codes	zebras
zoo cages	zoo keepers	xylophones

Copyright© Great Ideas For Teaching! ARTICULATION CURRICULUM I

Name _____ Date _____ Sound __Z__

In speech class: The words under each picture were said _____ times.
For homework: The words under each picture are to be said _____ times.
Additional instructions: _____
_____

Zeezee sees some bones.   Zeezee sees some cheese.   Zeezee sees some bananas.

Zeezee sees some pies.   Zeezee sees some eggs.   Zeezee sees some nails.

Zeezee sees some pens.   Zeezee sees some noses.   Zeezee sees some toes.

Copyright© Great Ideas For Teaching!   ARTICULATION CURRICULUM I

Name _____ Date _____ Sound __ch__

In speech class: The word under each picture was said _____ times.
For homework: The word under each picture is to be said _____ times.
Additional instructions: _____
_____

chipmunk

chimney

chalkboard

chain

check mark

chair

chin

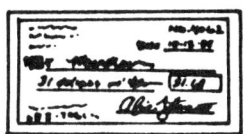
check

chicken leg

Copyright© Great Ideas For Teaching!   ARTICULATION CURRICULUM I

Name _____ Date _____ Sound __ch__

In speech class: The words under each picture were said _____ times.
For homework: The words under each picture are to be said _____ times.
Additional instructions: _____
_____

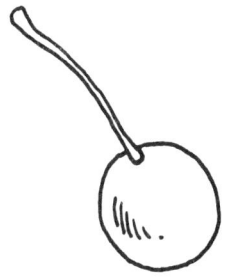
Choose a cherry.

Choose a chest.

Choose children.

Choose a chicken.

Choose chewing gum.

Choose a child.

Choose a cheerleader.

Choose a chief.

Choose cheese.

Copyright© Great Ideas For Teaching! ARTICULATION CURRICULUM I

Name _____ Date _____ Sound __ch__

In speech class: The words under each picture were said _____ times.

For homework: The words under each picture are to be said _____ times.

Additional instructions: _____
_____

a check on a chipmunk

a check on a chimney

a check on a chalkboard

a check on a chain

a check on a check

a check on a chair

a check on a chin

a check on a chief

a check on a chicken leg

Copyright© Great Ideas For Teaching!   ARTICULATION CURRICULUM I

Name _____ Date _____ Sound __ch__

In speech class: The words under each picture were said _____ times.
For homework: The words under each picture are to be said _____ times.
Additional instructions: _____
_____

a cherry on a chair

a chest on a chair

children on a chair

a chicken on a chair

chewing gum on a chair

a child on a chair

a chief on a chair

a cheerleader on a chair

cheese on a chair

Copyright© Great Ideas For Teaching! ARTICULATION CURRICULUM I

Name _____ Date _____ Sound **ch**

In speech class: The words under <u>each</u> picture were said _____ times.

For homework: The words under <u>each</u> picture are to be said _____ times.

Additional instructions: _____
_____

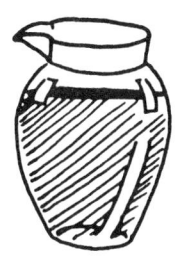
Touch a pitcher.

Touch a butcher.

Touch a kitchen.

Touch a teacher.

Touch a pitcher.

Touch a rocking chair.

Touch a hatchet.

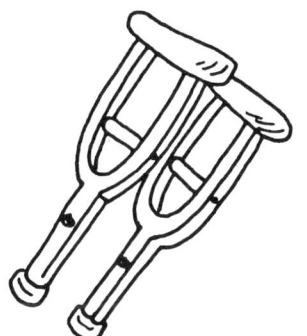
Touch crutches.

Touch matches.

Copyright© Great Ideas For Teaching!   <u>ARTICULATION CURRICULUM I</u>

Name _____ Date _____ Sound __ch__

In speech class: The words under <u>each</u> picture were said _____ times.

For homework: The words under <u>each</u> picture are to be said _____ times.

Additional instructions: _____
_____

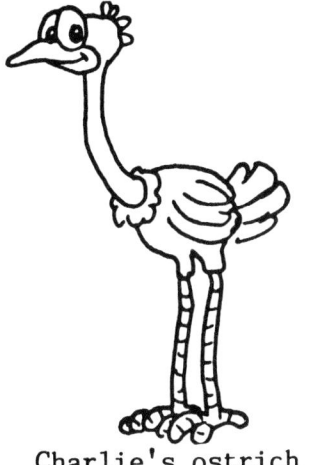
Charlie's ostrich

Charlie's patch

Charlie's church

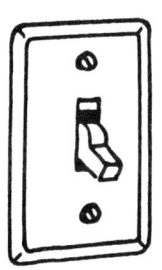
Charlie's switch

Charlie's watch

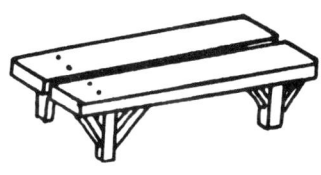
Charlie's bench

Charlie's witch

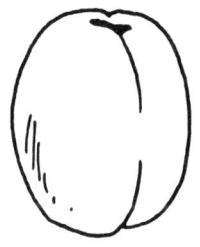
Charlie's peach

Charlie's match

Copyright© Great Ideas For Teaching!   <u>ARTICULATION CURRICULUM I</u>

Name _____ Date _____ Sound __sh__

In speech class: The word under <u>each</u> picture was said _____ times.
For homework: The word under <u>each</u> picture is to be said _____ times.
Additional instructions: _____
_____

shirt

shawl

shell

ship

sugar

shadow

sheep

shamrock

shield

Copyright© Great Ideas For Teaching!   <u>ARTICULATION CURRICULUM I</u>

Name _____ Date _____ Sound __sh__

In speech class: The words under <u>each</u> picture were said _____ times.
For homework: The words under <u>each</u> picture are to be said _____ times.
Additional instructions: _____
_____

Shout, shout!

Shampoo, shampoo!

Show, show!

Shake, shake!

Shuffle, shuffle!

Shut, shut!

Shower, shower!

Shoot, shoot!

Shine, shine!

Copyright© Great Ideas For Teaching!   ARTICULATION CURRICULUM I

Name _____ Date _____ Sound **sh**

In speech class: The words under <u>each</u> picture were said _____ times.

For homework: The words under <u>each</u> picture are to be said _____ times.

Additional instructions: _____
_____

She has a shovel.

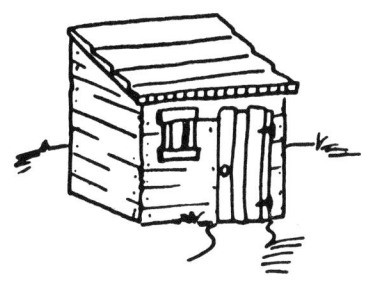

She has a shed.

She has shutters.

She has a shower.

She has a shade.

She has a shelf.

She has a shark.

She has a sheriff.

She has a shoe.

Copyright© Great Ideas For Teaching! ARTICULATION CURRICULUM I

Name _____ Date _____ Sound __sh__

In speech class: The words under each picture were said _____ times.
For homework: The words under each picture are to be said _____ times.
Additional instructions: _____
_____

Shannon sees a shoe box.

Shannon sees shoestrings.

Shannon sees a shoulder.

Shannon sees a sheet.

Shannon sees shampoo.

Shannon sees shears.

Shannon sees a shade tree.

Shannon sees a shy boy.

Shannon sees a sharp knife.

Copyright© Great Ideas For Teaching!   ARTICULATION CURRICULUM I

Name _____ Date _____ Sound **sh**

In speech class: The words under each picture were said _____ times.

For homework: The words under each picture are to be said _____ times.

Additional instructions: _____
_____

I wish I had a horseshoe.

I wish I had a wishbone.

I wish I had a pencil sharpener.

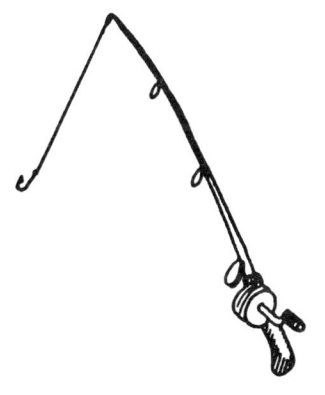
I wish I had a fishing pole.

I wish I had dishes.

I wish I had a washing machine.

I wish I had a mushroom.

I wish I had a saltshaker.

I wish I had a parachute.

Copyright© Great Ideas For Teaching!   ARTICULATION CURRICULUM I

Name _____ Date _____ Sound __**sh**__

In speech class: The words under <u>each</u> picture were said _____ times.

For homework: The words under <u>each</u> picture are to be said _____ times.

Additional instructions: _____
_____

Show me a brush.

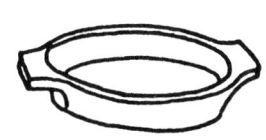
Show me a dish.

Show me a starfish.

Show me a hairbrush.

Show me a fish.

Show me a toothbrush.

Show me a bush.

Show me a radish.

Show me a shoe brush.

Copyright© Great Ideas For Teaching!   ARTICULATION CURRICULUM I

Name _____ Date _____ Sound **th** ___

In speech class: The words under <u>each</u> picture were said _____ times.

For homework: The words under <u>each</u> picture are to be said _____ times.

Additional instructions: _____

_____

thimble

thank-you note

thermometer

thumb

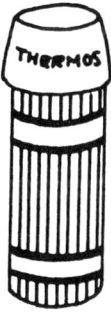

thermos

thorns

three

thirteen

thread

Copyright© Great Ideas For Teaching! ARTICULATION CURRICULUM I

Name _____ Date _____ Sound __th__

In speech class: The word under each picture was said _____ times.

For homework: The word under each picture is to be said _____ times.

Additional instructions: _____
_____

throne	throat	thief
throw	thatched roof	thermometer
thunder	Thanksgiving	thumbtack

Copyright© Great Ideas For Teaching!   ARTICULATION CURRICULUM I

Name _____ Date _____ Sound __t h__

In speech class: The words under each picture were said _____ times.

For homework: The words under each picture are to be said _____ times.

Additional instructions: _____
_____

 Think of a thimble.

 Think of a thank-you note.

 Think of a thermometer.

 Think of a thumb.

 Think of a thermos.

 Think of thorns.

 Think of a three.

 Think of a thirteen.

 Think of thread.

Copyright© Great Ideas For Teaching!   ARTICULATION CURRICULUM I

Name _____ Date _____ Sound __**th**__

In speech class: The words under <u>each</u> picture were said _____ times.

For homework: The words under <u>each</u> picture are to be said _____ times.

Additional instructions: _____
_____

That is a throne.

That is a throat.

That is a thief.

That is throw.

That is a thatched roof.

That is a thermometer.

That is thunder.

That is Thanksgiving.

That is a thumbtack.

Copyright© Great Ideas For Teaching! ARTICULATION CURRICULUM I

Name _____ Date _____ Sound **th**

In speech class: The words under each picture were said _____ times.

For homework: The words under each picture are to be said _____ times.

Additional instructions: _____
_____

Thelma's mother	Thelma's father	Thelma's bathtub
Thelma's toothbrush	Thelma's toothpicks	Thelma's birthday cake

Thelma's toothpaste

Thelma's bathrobe

Thelma's panther

Copyright© Great Ideas For Teaching!   ARTICULATION CURRICULUM I

Name _____ Date _____ Sound __**th**__

In speech class: The words under <u>each</u> picture were said _____ times.

For homework: The words under <u>each</u> picture are to be said _____ times.

Additional instructions: _____
_____

This is a wreath.

This is a mouth.

This is a cloth.

This is a tooth.

This is a path.

This is north.

This is a moth.

This is a washcloth.

This is the earth.

Copyright© Great Ideas For Teaching!   ARTICULATION CURRICULUM I